Cryptozarkia

Mark Spitzer

RELATED WORKS BY MARK SPITZER

In Search of Monster Fish, University of Nebraska Press, 2019

Beautifully Grotesque Fish of the American West, University of Nebraska Press, 2017

GLURK! A Hellbender Odyssey, Anaphora Literary Press, 2016

Return of the Gar, University of North Texas Press, 2015

Crypto-Arkansas, Spuyten Duyvil, 2013

Season of the Gar, University of Arkansas Press, 2010

Cryptozarkia

Mark Spitzer

Cornerpost Press | 2023

ISBN: 979-8-218-12232-4

Library of Congress Control Number: 2022951546

Edited by Mark Spitzer and Phillip Howerton

Cover design by Phillip Howerton and Ronald Kerns

Interior design by Mark Spitzer and Phillip Howerton

Cornerpost Press
214 West Maple
West Plains, MO 65775
www.cornerpostpress.com

Acknowledgments

"Hoop Snake Hype" published in *Elder Mountain: A Journal of Ozark Studies.*

"Goggle-Eye Gobbledygook," "Ozark Howler Apocrypha," and "Howladdendum" published in *Supernatural Studies: An Interdisciplinary Journal of Art, Media, and Culture.*

"Goggle-Eye Gobbledygook," "Big Al: The Name Remains," and "Old Blue Possibilities" anthologized in *Wild Muse: Ozarks Nature Poetry* from Cornerstone Press.

"Goggle-Eye Gobbledygook" and "Hoop Snake Hype" published in *Cave Region Review.*

Thanks to: The annual Ozarks Symposium at Missouri State—West Plains where a few of these studies were presented and others found inspiration; nieces Annalee and Eleanor Bailey for monster-hunting the Ozark Howler, finding clues I missed, and hearing the initial hooing; Brock Watson for info on Fayetteville howlery; Destany Lytle, Ben "Minnow Bucket" Daamgard and Gene Daamgard for guidance and good company in the Ozark underworld; Eric "Hippy" Tumminia and Lea Graham for insight into Scottish American culture in the Ozarks; Karen Pruneda and the Interlibrary Loan staff at Torreyson Library at the University of Central Arkansas for obtaining old newspaper articles and ordering relevant publications; dependable research assistant Scotty Lewis for digging through files and keeping it unreal 1300 miles away; everyone who led me to sources and granted permission to use photos and information; all blurbers and reviewers; and Phillip Howerton and Cornerstone Press for showcasing contemporary Ozark genius up in them hills.

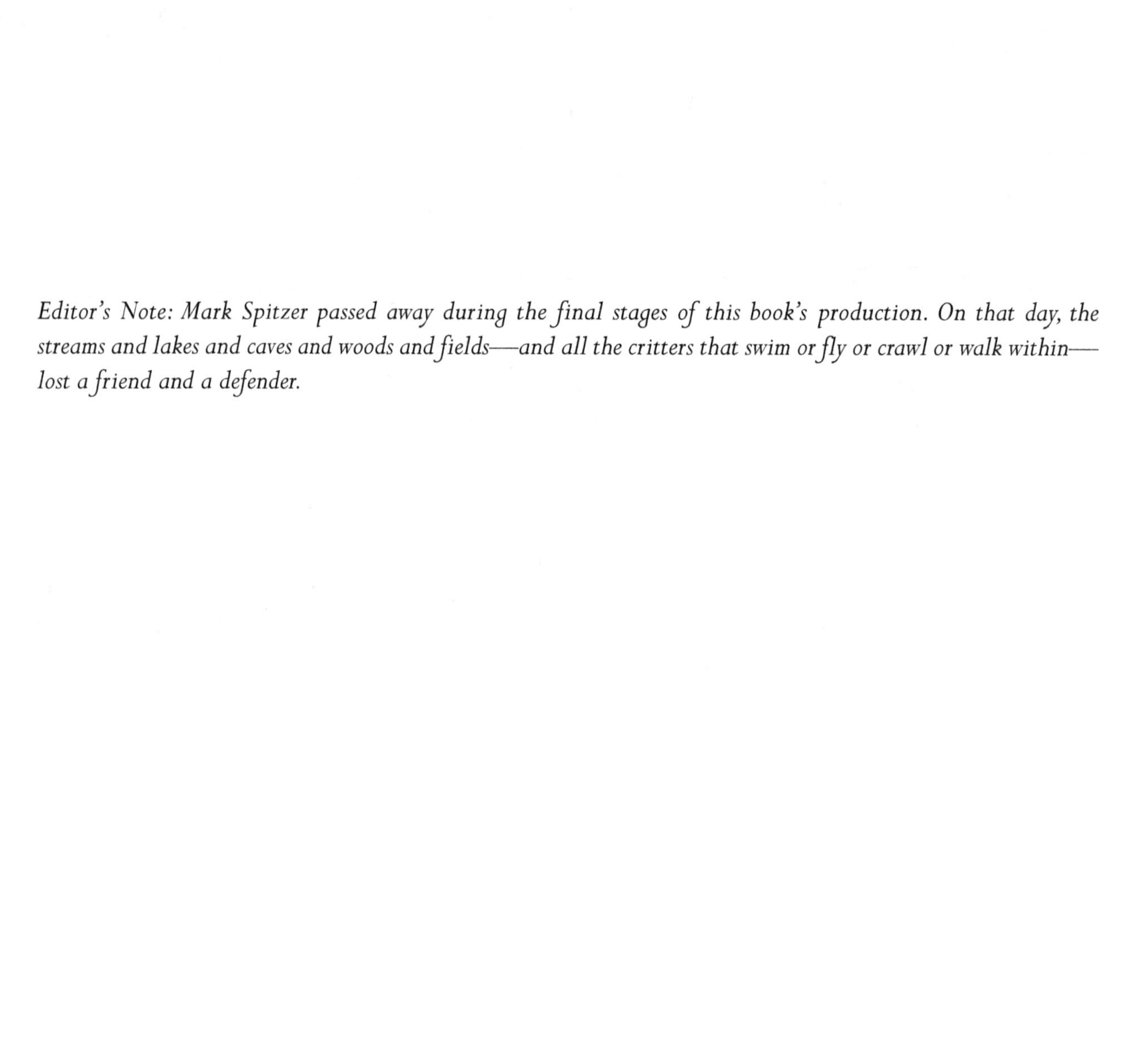

Editor's Note: Mark Spitzer passed away during the final stages of this book's production. On that day, the streams and lakes and caves and woods and fields—and all the critters that swim or fly or crawl or walk within— lost a friend and a defender.

Preface

Legendary cryptozoological creatures have found fertile ground to evolve in the Ozark Mountains, and I've had a blast researching such phenomena. I look for the stories behind the stories, then report my findings via the Postmodern technique of "investigative poetry," an obscure American literary practice sometimes referred to as "documentary poetry" or "docupoetry," which finds its roots in the poetics of Ezra Pound, Charles Olson, William Carlos Williams, and Ed Sanders. Through a semi-scholarly but not unbiased collaging of folklore, history, biology, journalism, politics, imagery, and literary truncations from myriad texts, these nonfiction exposés on hoop snakes, wampus cats, the Ozark Howler, the enigmatic blue humans of Blowing Cave, the intangible Blue Man of Spring Creek, and more are now documented in free verse with direct citations and commentary gained from first-person fieldwork. These studies and others comprise *Cryptozarkia,* which is envisioned as a companion volume to *Crypto-Arkansas*.

Meanwhile, colorful cultural narratives exist in the Ozarks, and plenty unexplained monstrifications from our collective consciousness continue to ignite imaginations. I'm grateful to those who contributed to such tall tales in the story-telling tradition of old timers amusing the truly inquisitive. As for those, however, who have tried to deceive, or who have rehashed crackpot rumors so as to rub their palms and chuckle from a distance, I see such insincerity as lacking integrity. At this point, we don't need any more manufactured BS in the mix, which isn't helpful in understanding the psychology of why we project human and anti-human qualities unto fantastic fusions.

What is helpful is digging up the lost details, interrogating deviations from the norm, and continuing to investigate narratives that strive to make sense of our relationships with the natural world.

Mark Spitzer
In the Ozark Foothills
2022

Table of Contents

Hoop Snake Hype

Hoop Snake Hype

Of all the suspect Ozark malarkey
the hogwash of the hoop snake
has got to be called out

supposedly
there's a certain serpent up in them hills
which grips its tail in its jaws
forms itself into a circle
then goes rolling at speeds
exceeding sixty miles per hour   (Museum of Hoaxes)
before straightening out
at the last second
and skewering humans
with the deadly stinger
on its tail

of course
there are a few ways to avoid
this type of attack
first documented in
the 1700s   (*Tour in the U.S.A.* Vol. I, 1784)
then later recounted
in tales of Paul Bunyon
and Pecos Bill

first
you can dive through
a hoop snake's hoop
which will cause it to high
tail it away

or secondly
and most commonly
as Vance Randolph described:
    "in most cases
        this creature pursues some poor hillman
        misses him, and strikes the horn on its tail
        into a growing tree;
        the hoop snake's horn is deadly poison
        and the tree always dies"
                                    (Ozark Magic and Folklore, 1947, 254)

Otto Rayburn adds to this
the story of Aunt Steller Bonham
who "wus pickin' blackberries
        on a bluff above Clabber Crick . . .
        [and] saw a hoop snake rollin' straight fer her.
        Snakes alive, she wus scairt!
        Hit wus as big 'round as yer arm
        an' made a loop th' size of a bar'l hoop"

that hoop snake   though
    "jist ripped her dress
     with th' pint of hits tail"
and when she washed that dress
    "th' pizen in hit turned
      three tubs o' warsh water
      plumb green"
                                            (Ozark Country, 1941)

(bonus fact:
hoop snake venom
has also been reported
to make wood expand
to improbable
proportions)

Anyway
in the oral tradition of the hill folk
more hoopy hearsay
began going viral;
a phenom which continues
                to this day
    especially in
                chatroom chatter

ie
South Carolina 2009
when Norma Nichols posted
how her and her grandma fled
an aggressive
            rotating
                    wheel of a snake
            adding
                "THEY ARE REAL"

similarly
Vietnam vet Darrell C
swore "a hoop snake stung [his grandpa]
thrashing wheat in Oklahoma"
1917

then there's Kaijene
whose "grampa died from a bite in 1960"
as well as Wendell Davis recalling
one "the size of a . . . bicycle tire"   (hoaxes.org)

that's why
back in the thirties
herpetologist Raymond Ditmars
placed "$10,000 in a trust at a New York bank
         as a prize to be given to the first person
         providing evidence"   (snake-facts.weebly.com)

but guess what?
No one brought
a hoop snake in

so let's break it down
to the most common denominator
in most of these stories:
the claim
this snake
is black

         a detail noted
by reptile curator Karl Schmidt
of the Field Museum of Natural History:
         "the habit of the common black snake of eastern North America
            of gliding along at great speed over the tops of bushes
            without descending to the ground
            may have a bearing on the origin of
            the belief in the hoop snake's
            rolling method of progression"   (*Natural History Magazine,* 1925)

a fact I can corroborate
having witnessed on the Fourche-LaFave near Bigelow
          a six foot black rat snake
          (*Pantherophis obsoletus*)
flying down a cliff face
hardly even touching it
in pursuit of a skittering mole

I won't go so far   however
as to say its form was circular;
if anything it
                was a constricting
                                contracting
              letter S

but with every leaping
                looping
                        lunge for lunch
        while coiling and uncoiling
                        and blasting like a lightning flash
                it kept creating
                        an opening
                                and closing O

and that's how this myth came to exist
in Arkansas and everywhere
where Eve's apple
is still an issue

        with few inclined
to set the record straight.

Goggle-Eye Gobbledygook

Goggle-Eye Gobbledygook

According to *Rayburn's Ozark Guide*
a publication that used to print
"tall tales or other bits of lore"   (Spring 1951)
there was this professor from Kansas
who went fishing on the Buffalo River
circa 1917

now this old boy
had "shell rim spectacles"
and he hooked "a fish so large
that he could not land it"
so he hung on and it
pulled him in

Yep   even to this day
folks have seen the professor
being dragged up and down the river
still clinging to his fishing pole

but wait   there's more
because suddenly there was
a new fish in town:
          Ambloplites rupestris
a non-native member of
          the sunfish family
built like a cross between
a bream and a bass
with a notable feature:

                    big ol' bubble eyes
just like that missing professor
with his thicker than baloney
                            bifocals
                            and refusal to let go

so now his haint inhabits the streams
of northeast Arkansas
where an introduced species
commonly known as "goggle-eye"
is believed to exist because
                            "all such fish
                                had seen the professor"   (Spring 1947)

in an area   by the way
that just happened to be stocked
with this specific
northern rock bass
            (which differs from the Ozark
              and shadow bass)
spawned in a hatchery
            "established in Neosho, Missouri"   (Cashner and Suttkus, 1978)
              à la 1888

So is it a coincidence
that most federal stocking activities
take decades for breeding
populations to take

or is it a fact that
    "great numbers of fish
      soon appeared in the river . . .
      with protruding eyes,
      resembling . . . the Kansas professor"?   (*Ozark Guide*, Spring 1947)

Well   Will Rice of St. Joe would know
because he's the journalist
who recorded the legend of this fish
            among other
            questionable
            contentions

eg   "a turtle killed in the Buffalo River . . .
which 'made a meal for forty families,
with two barrels of soup left over'"   (*We Always Lie to Strangers,* 1951, 69)

or the killer turnips that erupted from a shed
murdering a herd of cows   (*Ibid.,* 90)

or get this
"a man on [the] Buffalo River
who 'grabbed a big frog by the leg.
[which] jumped clear across the river
with him hanging on'"   (*Ibid.,* 71)

Let it be known   however
that Will Rice "was best known . . . for his sly humor.
            He didn't think of his yarns as tall tales,
            but liked to consider them
            'things that are always possible—
            but not always very probable'"   (*Arkansas Gazette,* April 6, 1953)

in his own words
Will Rice of St. Joe wrote
      "I always enjoyed seeing the town's name . . .
      so I began sending items from here
      just to see 'St. Joe' in print"

  adding
      "Sometimes, perhaps,
      I would help the item out . . .
      to make it more entertaining
      and to insure a wider circulation"

(Arkansas Democrat Sunday
Magazine, July 18, 1948)

So no wonder a year
after documenting this rise
      in goggle-eyes
Rice recycled his own
fishy fish story

"about the phantom fisherman . . .
 a determined looking professor from Kansas with . . .
 horn-rimmed glasses"
      who hooked a catfish in Arkansas
      weighing 400 pounds
      et cetera
      et cetera

So now his ghost sits fishing there
and they say that during electrical storms
      "the haunted fisherman throws
      fish over his shoulder
      and the person who happens to be there
      can fill a basket"

(Ibid., April 11, 1948)

Anyway
that's the news from St. Joe where
the apparitions of imaginations
        still hold to claims made
by dubious Ozark storytellers

like those who spin yarns
of goggle-eyed perch
infused with the spirit
of a stubborn professor
        still being towed
            up and down the Buffalo River

an unlikely story
that keeps getting told

        one way
or another.

The Maddening of Wampus Lore:
Evolution of a Wildcat Trope

The Maddening of Wampus Lore: Evolution of a Wildcat Trope

> "wampus: a strange, objectionable, or
> monstrous person or thing"
> —*Merriam Webster*

> "catawampus: out of alignment, in disarray
> or disorder: crooked, askew"
> —*Wiktionary*

Like pretty much all
legends of crypto
creatures specific
to this social experiment
  the idea was thunk up
  by Native Americans

the myth of the Ewah,
    Evil Demon of Madness,
started with the Cherokee
who appropriated some pre-Columbian
human/hybrid jaguar tales
from Aztec/Maya/Olmec cultures
dating back to 1200 BC

(thehistorybandits.com)

the story is a suspicious wife
donned a wily wildcat hide
to spy on her husband
performing sacred tribal magic

since this was forbidden
an incensed medicine man
transformed "her into a terrible monster—
       half woman and half mountain cat . . .
       doomed to roam the hills
       howling desolately"   (americanfolklore.net)

after that
the storylines kept evolving
in Appalachia   for example
a brave named Standing Bear
went looney tunes due
to the Ewah driving
dudes insane

his vengeful wife Running Deer
then put on a bobcat mask
applied "a black paste to hide her scent"
and freaked the hell
out of the Ewah

     who was not amused
at being punked
& so he put a curse on her

       thus
Running Deer's "spirit
now inhabits the Wampus Cat"   (grunge.com)

predictably
Whitey then hopped on the wampus wagon
with news reports of colossal
cattle killing cougars
coming out of the Carolinas   (*Mooresville Enterprise*, 1931)

meanwhile
a conspiracy of Alabamans
claimed the US government
had invented a top secret
wampular mashup
of a mountain lion and a wolf
to serve as a wartime
courier   (*McDowell News*, July 29, 2009)

consequently
in the mid twentieth century
diverse subspecies were documented
starting with the Whistling Wampus
        "an immense black cat with supernatural intelligence
            which lured woodsmen to their doom
            by whistling at them from dark cedar thickets"   (*We Always Lie to Strangers*, 58–59)

the Whistler   as it's also known,
        "a blood-thirsty animal . . . found only in
            the wildest sections of the Ozarks,"   (*Strange Customs of the Ozark Hillbilly*, 1947)
was notorious for climbing down chimneys
in pursuit of lactose lapping babies
when shrieking screams
slashed the night

noises later
conjectured to be steamboats
screeching on the rivers

then there's the Wowzer
                    or Woozer
        "a kind of super-painter"
(that's Ozarkian for "panther")
            "five or six times the size
            of an ordinary mountain lion"
which goes around
biting heads off
horses and cows

a more amphibious variant
is the Great Gallywampus
which "swims like a colossal mink"   (*We Always Lie to Strangers*, 58–59)
            when it's not out
massacring livestock

other wampy felines include
Hoo-Hoos and Whoo-Hoos
Hickelsnoopuses and Ring-Tailed Tooters
and the Side-Hill variety
with longer legs on one side
for walking along
mountain tops

then there's your standard
six-legged model
        "four to run and two to fight"   (conwaywampuscats.com)

and the rarer Canadian
eight-wheeled version
          "four atop and four beneath
            so as to always land feet first"   *(Canadian National Railways Magazine*, 1929)

to the point that
the reputation of the wampus cat
has been firmly established
as a "howling, evil creature with yellow eyes
        that can . . . pierce the hearts and souls of those
        unfortunate enough to cross its path"   (appalachianhistory.net)

So why all these varying wampii?
Well   as explained by the author
of "Catching a Wampus
Cat By Its Tale"
            "Every storyteller puts the tale
              into different words and adds
              some of their own
              imagination.

              Accordingly
              this can often lead
              to some highly remarkable
              contradictions"   (fearsomecritters.org)

which   I should add
only contradict each other because
the more cattywampus stories there are
the more cattywampus factors there are
that can't be
verified.

Big Al:
The Name Remains

BIG AL

Big Al: The Name Remains

As Ernest Dewcy wrote
in an article entitled
      "A Lot of Strange Creatures
        Are Lying About the Ozarks Area":

      "It has been noted that
      sterility of the soil
      has a strong tendency
      to increase fertility
      of the imagination"

(The Hutchinson News-Herald,
May 13, 1951)

which accounts for legends like Big Al
a monstrous alligator gar
native to the White River
and allegedly not a
      "'natural' gar at all,
        but some kind of a demon
        in disguise"

but the thing is
rumors of this "immortal . . .
          supernatural"
          thirty foot
          gargantugar

originated in the fields fringing
the Arkansas and Mississippi river valleys
from Natchez to Little Rock
following Reconstruction

still   not much is known
about this crypto boogey creature
other than it's been reported
        "to have killed many swimmers"
and was especially fond
        "of Negro children"

as Vance Randolph notes
        "when a young woman mysteriously disappeared
        the neighbors used to say
        'Big Al must have got her,'
        meaning that she had run off
        with a stranger"

                                                    (*We Always Lie to Strangers,* 206–207)

about the only other literal mention
                    of this mystery fish
is in a Baptist college honors thesis
focused on folk narratives
as constructs of communities

its author Sharon Hibbard states:
        "The folktale arises from a need
        experienced at a certain stage of development
        in human society.
        It is the circumstances
        which generate a folktale,
        which form its conception
        its shape,
        and its narrative style;
        as long as these circumstances prevail,
        the folktale will endure"

                                                    ("Folklore: A Study and
                                                    Tales from the Ozarks," 1975)

But the story of Big Al
did not endure
          it fizzled away
          with nary a trace

though one thing remained
a name whose legacy can be found
              in American mobsters
Big Al Bruno and Big Al Capone

and numerous athletes and musicians
not to mention professional wrestlers
              comedians and
race car drivers

there's also Big Al
the fossilized Allosaurus
Big Al the mascot
for Alabama's Crimson Tide
and Big Al's strip club
the first topless bar
in the USA

and let's not forget
Big Gay Al from *South Park*
Big Al as code for Alzheimer's
and a renowned
              thousand pound
                   Big Al
                        igator in Texas

but there are also plenty massive fish
with this lasting moniker
like the loveable lunker in Andrew Clements'
bestselling children's book
Big Al   (Simon & Schuster, 1997)

plus a famous "neurotic" triggerfish   (proquest-com.ucark.idm.oclc.org/central/docview/
at Boston's New England Aquarium   268812266/2F03F7427D054668PQ/2)
who made national news
when it outgrew
its tank

then there's the iconic champion bass
worth fifteen thousand cash
at the annual Forrest Wood Cup
Fishing Contest in Hot Springs
who "has only been caught once
        in 2017"
                                                (Arkansas Democrat-Gazette,
                                                        August 5, 2018)

So what do all these larger than life
mystical and mythical
Big Als have in common?

Answer:
as Higgins wrote
folk tales arise
from societal needs

like the need to create
        scapegoats
        saviors
        magical muses

whatever we need
that's bigger than us
stronger than us

and powerful enough
        to bullshit all
the bullshit away.

Ozark Howler Apocrypha

Ozark Howler Apocrypha

With all its snawfuses
            bingbuffers
            and random snickelhoopuses
you'd think Arkansas would have enough
fictitious creatures in its cache
of debatable obscurities

but then here comes the Ozark Howler
known for its plasma-curdling scream
sometimes described as "somewhere between
a wolf's howl and an elk's bugle"   (417escapeartist.com)

            or
as described in *Tales
of the Ozark Howler*
            "It had a kind of voice to it,
              but another tone as well,
              one that was practically mineral.
              It sounded like the screech of an animal,
              but also like a metal blade
              being scraped over an unmoving stone"   (Ashton, 2019)

This description comes from a book
allegedly "published in 1936
            by a small, local printer
            shortly before the death of its author"
            Saul Ashton   (no info on him anywhere)

who supposedly collected
"folktales, eyewitness accounts,
[and] archival documents"   (abe.books.com)
          in a posthumous study pulled from distribution
          by scandalized family members
          who couldn't condone
          such an unchristian
          abomination

Then came editor Hawthorne Cornus
          an identity just as bogus
who reprinted Ashton in 2019
in a self-published paperback
that's been effective
in continuing the conspiracy

of a difficult to identify
cross between a large cat and bear
          with a side of canine,
red "glowing eyes and horns"
and a shaggy form
that "most agree . . .
          is black"   (exploresouthernhistory.com)

But seriously folks
the Nightshade Bear   as it's also known
was inspired by tales from the 1800s
of Daniel Boone shooting some sort
of unknown hybrid

which later merged with English hellhounds
all mixed up with wampus cats
and a dash of Native
American lore

until "journalist Lisa Leigh exposed a double hoax . . .
        when rumors were spread . . . by Bigfoot enthusiasts,
        seeking to portray the Ozark Howler as . . .
        invented by a student at
        the University of Arkansas"
        1994

according to Leigh
    "This student was said to have made a bet with members of a rival fraternity
    that he could convince the local NBC affiliate to run a story . . . .
    [but the] student was never identified . . . .
    [and] in the classic style of urban legends . . . .
    the name of the fraternity . . .
    was never specified"   (ozarkhowler.net)

        Still
the sketchy student story took off
just like the internet
"early in 1998"

when an alias named Jonathan Cook
          began a sham email campaign
          infiltrated chatroom chatter
          and set up deceptive
          web pages

before confessing to cryptozoologist Loren Coleman
that he "wondered what would happen
          if he created a 'new cryptid'"   (cryptomundo.com)

After that
a few more sightings were reported
in Rolla MO and Springdale AR

but the one that stuck
came from Devil's Den State Park
on the outskirts of Fayetteville
2015

seems electrician John Meyers
was camping when he witnessed
some mutt with antlers and an extra long tail
so took a series of photographs
that had no trouble
going viral

the state game and fish commish   however
declared this howler a Photoshopped hoax
even though Meyers swore on the Lord
that his pics were legit

I therefore recruited
two local monster hunters
nieces Annalee and Eleanor
and we hit the Yellow Rock Trail
because that's where it
was last spotted

it didn't take long
to find a murdered bird
next to a tree with three
                deep
            claw marks in it

(Springfield News-Leader,
December 15, 2015)

hardly evidence enough
        to stake a solid claim
but then we heard a high faint wail
coming from the valley below

where Meyers had taken
photographs

and I kid you not
that scream sounded
                    like two
                              long
                                   lingering
                                             *Hooooooo*s

as in the Hoo-Hoo
    another name
for the Howler

in fact
down in Gurdon Arkansas
just south of the Ouachitas
there's the International
Hoo-Hoo Headquarters and Museum
        "founded in 1892
            [by] the Concatenated Order of Hoo-Hoo . . .
            [a] fraternal organization of lumbermen
            and those in trades related
            to the lumber industry"   (Arkansas.com)

because
as noted by Vance Randolph
lumberjacks were "vulnerable to attack . . .
                working . . . smack dab in the middle
                of Ozark Howler habitat"

hence
a "secret society" was created
to protect "lumbermen
all over America"   (ozarkhowlers.com)

Anyhoo
the girls and I
began hooooing back
and we received a few
hooos in response

it must be remembered though
that the campsites below were full of families
hiking and swimming and retelling stories
        of wampus cats
        and bigfoots and
        howlers howling
        in the night

but it wasn't night
it was the morning
and the howls we heard
were coming from a community
where a certain headline
must be considered:

        "Howls Heard Around Fayetteville
          During Quarantine Trend"

followed by
the following sentence:

"People are walking out the door each night at 8 p.m.
to give a howl and feel a sense of togetherness."

(5newsonline.com,
April 3, 2020)

meaning
this population
had been preconditioned
to hooooo like
Hoo-Hoos do

and that   fellow monster enthusiasts
is the no fun but
objective truth

in a who's who
of Hoo-Hoo
hooey.

Howladdendum

Howladdendum

While investigating *Ozark Howler Verse:*
                Poems of the Dark Beast
the only full length collection of poetry
focused on this mythic cryptid

I suddenly saw
some curious
connections

First of all
this book was self-published in 2019
by the exact same
POD company   (KDP in South Carolina)
that put out Ashton's fraudulent
        Tales of the Ozark Howler
with the exact same font
on the covers and in text

Secondly
it's obvious that one of these books
served as a template for the other
the prelim and copyright pages
table of contents and author's bio
all set up in the same order
with the same conventions
for headers and page numbering

not only that
but the bios take the same approach
for framing and phrasing
using humor and innuendo to mask
a lack of traceable
          information

Ergo
it can be established
that the pseudonym of Rufus Grey   (two names, two colors; rufus being red in Latin
is actually Hawthorne Cornus   two names, two trees; meaning there's
                                                                      a pattern here)

So no wonder in his intro
Cornus provides a shout-out to Grey
an optometrist living in Missouri
my ass!

for no such eye
doc exists
          in fact
Rufus Grey of Kansas City
    (aka   Rufus Gray with an A)
also bills himself as
"a fantasy fiction writer [who
has] . . . written about Asian mythology
and European legends"   (ozarkhowlers.com)

but good luck finding any other publications
by the penname of "Rufus Grey"
or "Hawthorne Cornus" for that matter
whose scholarship is just as elusive
as the fabled Ozark Howler

nonetheless
the anonymous host of ozarkhowlers.com
claims to have met Grey at a bookstore
thereby leading to
the only known interview
with this alleged author   ("The Hoggish Howler of Rufus Grey")

    Speaking of that website
    you'll also find some promo for it
    along with OzarkHowler.net
    and OzarkHowler.info
    at the very end
    of Rufus' book

    and if you visit those WordPress sites
    you'll clearly see
    they're designed the same
    stylistically:

    the same typeface
    the same layout
    the same art
    and the same links harking back
    to the work of
    charlatans

But back to the idea
of a poet optometrist
also practicing
fantasy fiction
which begs the question:
    What do fantasy writers do?

the answer being:
>   They create fictions
>   based on fantasies
>
>   and not always
>   on the page

Just like "Jonathan Cook"
of the 1994 U of A howler hoax
who confessed he had manufactured
>   "free web pages and e-mail accounts"
to see if "people would fall for it"   (cryptomundo.com)

which   apparently
has become a trend
in worldbuilding fantasies
for personal
>   snickering
>   gain

as reflected in the pompous
>   condescending
>   pseudo intellectual tone
of the first and last lines
of rhymester Rufus'
"Resource" page:

>   "Still here? Seriously, don't you have anything better to do? . . . .
>   The truth is not out there"   (Grey, 78)

which might be true
depending how you look at it

but one truth I will declare
is that Rufus Grey
is Hawthorne Cornus
is Saul Ashton
is OzarkHowlers
.com
.info
.everything

and he's yucking it up right now
because anyone who fancies a howler
has fallen into an elaborate trap
crafted by a failed
fantasy hack

But sometimes   admittedly
this prankster hits on something
and that's what
pisses me off

as in his poem "Hainted"
where he criticizes those who seek the truth
when they know they're chasing make-believe:
   "We always lie to strangers
   but we never used
   to play such fools
   the butt of our own pranks
   dishonoring our inherited hills."

                          (Ibid., 55)

which is precisely what
fifty shades of Grey has done
by disgracing the spirit
of Ozark folklore

            a tradition meant to fascinate
    rather than deceive

    through servers
    and software
    and digital platforms
    with no safeguards
    for mis and dis
    information

that's how a subpar poet
with nothing else better to do
    and the means to do it
created a bunch of bunk
which folks are still
eating up

and that

is pathetic.

Old Blue Possibilities

Old Blue Possibilities

As *Time Magazine* reported in the thirties
the "Biggest catfish in the world is Old Blue
    who inhabits the Missouri River
    and is so big he once got stuck
    trying to go through a canal lock" (August 17, 1931)

hence   a plethora of narratives
of divers delving under dams
encountering mega
monster cats

primarily
Old Blue who
Vance Randolph contends
lived in the Osage River
"for at least fifty years" (*We Always Lie to Strangers*, 216)

such that
even after that system was dammed
the stories continued

particularly those
of a "well-known Osage River boatman"
named Jerry English
who made it his mission
to catch the lauded lunkercat that

according to Skunk Hide Turner
and M. N. White of Warsaw M.O.
once jumped "the Bagnell Dam
            and traveled all the way to Louisville"   (*Ibid.*, 217)

Robert Gilmore
on the other hand
refers to Old Blue's removal
from Lake of the Ozarks
which caused the water level to drop
        "18 feet,
          leaving docks, marinas
          and boats stranded"   (*OzarksWatch*, Vol. IV, no. 3, 1991)

such cock and bull   of course
has roots in journalism
and dates back to the journals
of Lewis and Clark

who recounted a "large 'white' catfish,
            undoubtedly [a] blue . . .
            reaching 1.5 m in length"   (American Fisheries Society Symposium
                                                          proceedings, 1999)

a solid possibility given
that sixty years later
a "blue channel cat" was documented
  "just below Portland, Missouri"
weighing "315 lb"   (Heckmann, 1950)

mucho reports of unlikely blues
then followed from St. Joe
where the skeleton of
a massive cat named Turntable Jack
was reportedly found on a sandbar in 1899
measuring "14 feet from head to tail"

to the lower Osage where
        "several old rivermen . . . estimated"
        the weight of a catfish to be
        "in the neighborhood of 500 pounds"   (*Missouri Conservationist*, June 1947)

to Little Rock
        (a cat so huge that it contained
        a "200-pound catfish, three fat hogs,
        a yoke of oxen and
        an acre of burnt woods")   (*We Always Lie to Strangers*, 214)

a tradition which continued
into the twenty first century
when Kato "Mudcat" Mudger
supposedly captured
a "736-pound . . . Mekong giant catfish"
in the Mississippi

the photo of this fish   howev
containing "a size 37 boot"   (RiverBender.com)
is clearly a flathead
whose eyes would be smaller
if this wasn't a blatant act
of sloppy Photoshoppery

But what if we didn't
have all these plausibilities
for Old Blue and
his behemoth brethren?

And who would we be
if we didn't continue
ye old Euro tradition
of exaggerating mongo
           man-munching catfish
            dating back to the Middle Ages?   (see *In Search of Monster Fish*, 2019, 15–29)

Well   if you ask me
we wouldn't be we
we would be
unwe

      which ain't a possibility
so why even consider
adjusting our nature
when Nature made us
exactly this way?

Just like Old Blue
                who
according to the Kansas City *Star*
has been known to stick
                "his head out of the water"
                and wink   (January 8, 1941)

thereby leaving
the question to consider:
        at who
        and why?

After the Blue Humans

After the Blue Humans

I

Blowing Cave
near Cushman Arkansas
was a different type
of investigation

    the Ozark enigmas here
    were not spawned
    by nineteenth century settlers
    musing on mutant
    woodland creatures
    or aquatic anomalies

    meaning farmers sighting
    wampy hoopy hybrids or
    mashups from the natural world
        clashing avec
"civilization"

    but come instead
    from a much more recent
    literary trend

    of a world war era
    sci fi mania
    embedding itself
    in the communal
    hippocampus

I'm talking azure aliens with
        oversized noggins
        bubble eyes and
        ESP

straight from the pages
of *Amazing Stories*
        a fantasy mag from the forties
making for a new
        perverted
        oral tradition

of supernatural narratives
based on pulp
publications

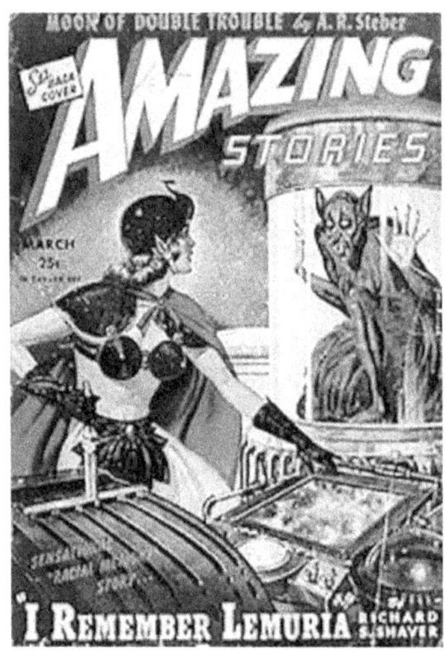

rather than the telephone game
of boogie cryptids
in our midst

Meanwhile
speleological
speculations
remain in the internet age
as enduring as
the cult of Q

(listing 8480590)

II

Thus our descent
into the maw
renowned for encounters
with "blue humans"

according to Land and Farm Real Estate
this "Native American archeological site
of significant historical importance
[with] thousands of Indian artifacts . . .

[is] famous for the spring fed creek . . .
and rooms containing lakes and waterfalls . . .
full of spirits . . . who made this a home"
nine thousand years ago

then
after eons of sacred
rituals and burials

came turn of the century
fancy dances
gala balls
and legends of lost
Confederate gold
complete with myths
of Jesse James

it was all before us
all below us
awaiting our literal
baptism

III

All helmeted, headlamped
and longjohned in polyester
we arrived in December:
Minnow Bucket
his brother Gene
& me

w/ Destany as our guide
a middle school teacher
children's author
and avid caver

all of us ready
to spelunk

IV

into the gorge
vast and gaping

past chiefs and elders
bulldozered over
to prevent further
pilfering

past twelve thousand years
of Dalton points
and other arrow
heads galore

now mudded under
centuries of graffitied stone
emblazoned by ravers
missing students
medevaced trespassers
and methed out outlaws
on the lam

to the padlocked gates
of innerworld lore
where Destany
held the key

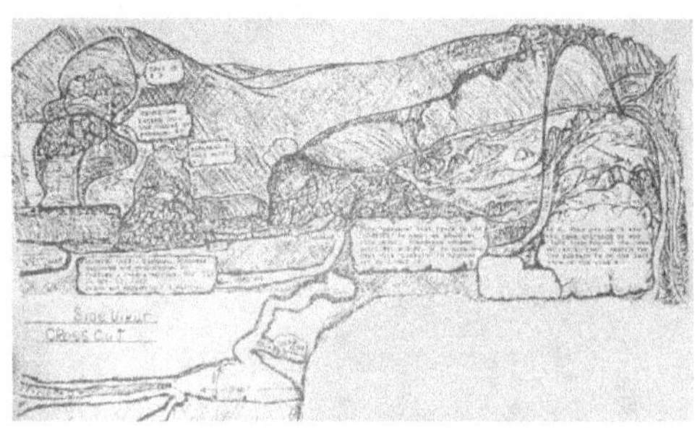

(*Shavertron*, Vol. 2)

V

down down
into the ground

    stalagmites
    stalactites
    an inscription from 19
    24

to a grand and glimmering
gilded cathedral
domed with living
        liquid
        fungi
           sparkling like iron pyrite

down down
into the bowels
of crystalline
conglomerations
random slabs
and rubble where

a secret path
through breakdown leads
to a passage dating back

to Edgar Rice Burroughs'
Pellucidar series
        popularized in the nineteen teens

the original "Hollow Earth" fiction
of monsters, mazeways
and ancient cities
filled with saber-tooth tigers
and naked maidens

an idea appropriated
decades later
by opportunist Richard Shaver

who populated this inner space
from outer space
with "Hobloks" sporting
        "pipe-stem arms and legs,
        pot bellies, [and] huge protruding eyes"   (*The Shaver Mystery, Book One,* 21)

and robots
        "standing erect on four short jointed legs"   (*Ibid.*, 32)

and snail men
        with "long, lumpy brown bod[ies]"   (*Ibid.*, 35)

and shades of Jabba
        the "great hulk Mula"   (*Ibid.*, 38)

plus freak species
        "hindquarters web-footed . . .
        [backs] maned with queer spines,"   (*Ibid.*, 66–67)
crazy old witches,
"dwarfish" beings,   (*Ibid.*, 91)
and bizarro things
with "rainbow wings"   (*Ibid.*, 115)

all embellished
by the once institutionalized mind
of a serialized
        paranormal
        space monkey
        junky

whose followers found a cave
so sought a connection
to his lore

        regardless if it's
fiction or not

VI

meanwhile
we kept delving
through crevices, cracks
splits & fissures

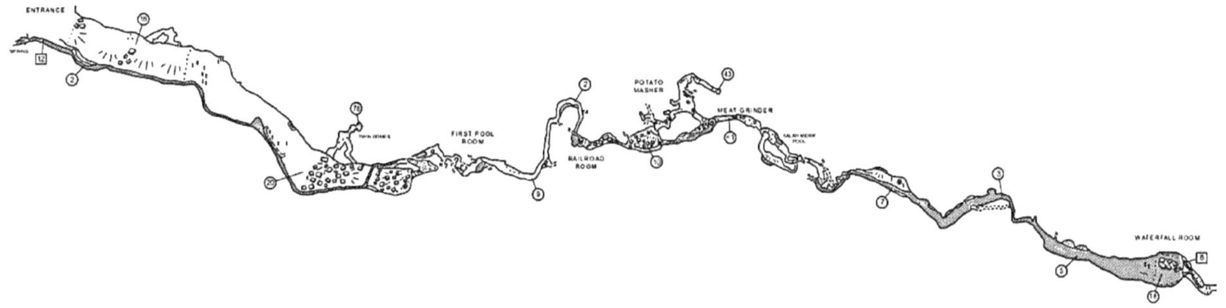

wrenching muscles
tearing tendons
squiggling in
and shimmying on

down down
into creepy
claustro town

visions of maddened
miners scrambling

flashes of earthquake
victims wailing

to the first pool room
of amphibious larvae
chilling in the trickle stream

17 to be exact
and 41 in the next;
data recorded
by Destany

In the past
reckless crews
just stomped on through
desecrating ponds of spawn

but now
Salamandria
rises again!

VII

According to the literature
an alias named Branton
published a book entitled
The Underground Empire

    which ain't available anywhere
except on a bunch of
self-published files
posted on a gratis website
    (the signature forum
of crypto shysters)

(derived from real name <u>Br</u>uce A<u>lan</u> Wal<u>ton</u>)

(no copyright date
whatsoever)

(angelfire.com/nm2/aona/branton2.html)

Anyway
    "the author of the Branton Files,
        a series of documents
        espousing various conspiracy theories"   (frankensaurus.com)

reported on an expedition
into Blowing Cave
in the fifties

where a "side passage" led
an unverified human named David L
to a "glass cave"
miles under crust

with George Wight
        (or "Wright"
        in other publications)
a bona fide
"UFO buff"   (facebook.com/377858655616927)

to a phosphorescent artery
where following a green fluorescence
        "they . . . found themselves face-to-face with a group of human-like beings who stood
        around 7 to 8 feet tall. 'Their' skin had a faint pale-bluish, almost clay-bluish tint to it and
        their eyes were relatively large and owl-like"

these "direct descendants of Noah"
communicated through
an "electronic 'translator'"
which divulged all sorts
of mind-blowing intel

that David L brought back to the surface
along with a "giant cave moth"
which abruptly crumbled into dust

Ultimately
these discoveries were revealed
to "the now late
Charles A. Marcoux"
while Wight/Wright
stayed below

According to Branton
"The peculiar thing about this incident . . . was that shortly after Wight had joined [the]
underground society all evidence and records of him ever existing began to mysteriously
disappear from the surface. Birth certificates, school records, computer records, bank
records, etc. all seemed to vanish, apparently the work of someone in a very influential
position who was able to erase all evidence that Wight had ever lived. Some researchers
still retain copies of George Wight's articles from the old UFO periodical, nevertheless.
This would open up the possibility that this underground race closely monitors events on
the surface, and even has 'workers' in various influential positions who act as mediators in
surface society."

(ufoexperiences.blogspot.com)

the result being
all this hoo-ha
posted in the nineties
found enough thrust
to spiral viral

which is how the blue humans
became another
Ozark attraction

for anyone willing
to forego logic

in favor of testing
the improbable Kool-Aid
of the fantastic

VIII

down

down

down

down

in and out
of the Railroad Room
with rusty spikes
nailed in walls
securing lines
for clamber climb

down

down

down

down

back in time
to the center of
the cavern mind

down

down

down

to the Potato Masher
a spasm chasm
of gastric contraction
dropping into
Oblivion

and down

and down

and down

another quarter mile
to the hamburgering of
the Meat Grinder

a nerve mashing
triangular passage
with a twenty two inch
hypotenuse

a brutal
bruising
birth canal
definitely not
for those who fear
the *SKRONCH* of being
skrunched alive

& down

& down

& down

& down

to the facts behind
apocrypha

IX

According to numerous secondhand sources
          "many people believed the [subworld] story . . .
             One of these believers was Charles Marcoux . . .
             [who] appears to have been told
             either by the mysterious David L or Mr. Wight
             that the Blowing Cave was an entrance to
             the underground world described by Shaver"   (drjbn.wordpress.com)

the details then
get muddled and confused:

Marcoux was said
to have led a trek in '66
in which contact was made
with the teros

             the "good" blue humans
             as opposed to the deros
             the "bad guys, so to speak"   (*Shavertron*, Vol. 2, 200)

Now flash forward to the eighties
when such narratives were distributed
through zines prompting
a surge in interest

all at a time
when Marcoux purportedly
held W[r]ight's "'lost' diary"   (*Ibid., 92*)
confirming Marcoux's rendezvous
with blue humans

Hence
"Marcoux and his wife
 moved to Cushman in 1983"
 with W[r]ight's notes and map
 and a team was formed
 to descend again

but while "visiting the land
around the cave"   (facebook.com/377858655616927)
Marcoux got stung
by a swarm of bees
        launching a fatal
        heart attack

the moral of this story being
any of the hypotheses
espoused by Shaver's
culture of absurdities

        ie
        "We are under mental control
         by underworld peoples using
         ancient telaug devices.

         Hitler was a puppet doing the telaug's bidding.
         Himmler . . . was following orders.
         And Stalin too."   (*Shavertron*, Vol. 2, 206)

        In other words
        take your pick
        of stupid shit

and pretend there's
an answer in it

X

down

down

down

further underground

into more
salamandy pools

both common cave (tangerine)
and dark-sided (brownish green)
but always speckled
with black spots

where slogging through
the waist deep current
sometimes stooping
sometimes slipping
but always aqua
ambulating

past ceilings studded
with lines of spiny
cicle teeth

thru chambers full
of flapping bats

and bright white
albinopedes

we heard the thrumming
hum of drums

along with vague
wavy voices
warbling from watersounds

distant drippings
plipping up

XI

* drip *

the Cold War notion of space aliens
being symbolic of "the Other"
is why the idea
of extraterrestrials
held such truck
during and after
McCarthyism

when comic book and sci fi covers
reflected an US v. them
mentality

* plip *

a thought I now
gotta reject
when considering the shamans
of Shaverism

whose disciples could hardly care less
about any state of politics

* drip *

for the amphibians were
as clear in the stream
as the fact that
for the creators of
blue humans

Marcoux
Wight / Wright
Branton
Palmer
Toronto
the whole bogus cast

the attraction's totally
juvenile

* plip *

cuz those ain't names
those are inventions
in it for
the same reason

D&D
roleplaying geeks
create kingdoms
because they can

* drip *

overgrown
  adolescents
    still living in
      their parent's basements

      though modern
        mythmakers
          definitely

          striving to leave
            a mark on something

XII

having cracked my skull
a couple times
reverberating shock
through noodle spine

with esophageal contortions
cramping up
adding to a weak kneed
wobble gut
that didn't need
no omeprazole in it

I pushed and pulled
and kept on wading
hunched and bent and
late for lunch
stomach full
of busted glass

a tearing
empty
sapping
suck

depleting me
of energy
and bringing on
the Chatterings

but pressing on
for a nuther half hour
gritting
clenching
grinding
dentine

we came upon
some moist formations
layered & labial

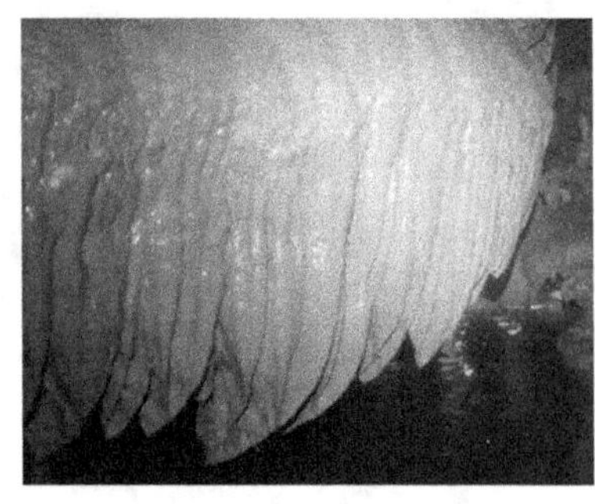

in a gray matter grotto
of scintillating shimmer-nodes
a new Faraway
begging question
of trogging on

but what can you do
when you can't turn back

and what if
cardiac

or broken leg
or strike of stroke

when there ain't no elevator
back to the top

and there ain't no cellular
service neither
and there sure as hell
ain't no wambulance
to be called?

so you swallow your terror
and force it down

XIII

Until Eureka!
the legendary lake
and waterfall—

a third to the heart
of the belly of the beast

and as far as my screeching
stomach would allow

so I sat down and ate
a PB&J

shivering and shuddering
      body temp
      plummeting

in the 58   degree stream
in the 58   degree air

where the chill remains
throughout the year

and it's evident that
the only blue human
in this abyss

is me

XIV

finally took a slug of water
which instantly untwisted
            intestinal pretzel

was woozy after that
stumbling drunken
      in psychotropic
      odyssey out

mashed an ankle
      in falling
      flailing
      trudge
      up

drips and plips
still sounding through
the corridors

XV

* drip *

Again the question
of what makes this quest
different than those
from the 1800s?

* plip *

an answer perhaps
in considering that

the oral tradition
is central to both

meaning retelling tales
of gowrows and gollywogs

is just as much an act
of storytelling
as proposing dodgy
blue humans

* drip *

Still   the straight up label
of "science fiction"
should make the latter
matter moot

* plip *

So why all these jokers
opting to believe
that Shaver & co
based fiction
on fact?

* drip *

answer being:

it's the same damn thing
it always is:

guys desiring
stuff to be thus

that is
we know what's up

but that's just not
sexy enough

* plip *

which is why we have
a culture of cults
whose right to remain ignorant
is enough to waste
all of us

consequently
being dreamers
they make junk up

cuz they can't
or won't
or refuse to see

the true amazing stories
really going on

in the true neural tunnels
of what's really going on

XVII

Personally
after descending into this underworld
and considering these scenarios
so crudely scrawled
on the cave walls
of amateur mass marketing

one's tolerance for make-believe
starts running low

especially when
those who want more
from the immeasurable more
we already have

is reason enough
to flabbergast God

So let's cut the horseshit, people
and get past the man
ufactured distractions
in this toxic
time of crisis

otherwise
we're just spelunking
nothing but our own
selfish
masturbations

of absolute
non-consequence

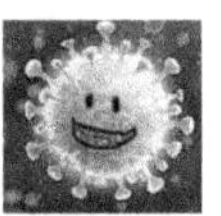

Tracking the Last American Wild Man

Tracking the Last American Wild Man

I

Back before the word "Sasquatch"
was coined by Canadian
J.W. Burns in the thirties   (*Canadian Encyclopedia*)

back before that iconic
Bigfoot photo went viral
     In '67

       thereby shaping modern model
       of stealthy jumbo primates
       existing in NorthAm wilderness

it was all about the medieval "wild man"
running through the woods
all hairy and half
nakedly raving

Basically
the settlers brought idea over
established concept on continent
and suddenly

the US and its upstairs neighbor
had its own evolution of
a common heretical
  Euro-demon
born from the Nordic
jack of the green

a leafy pagan
    vegetation spirit
that metamorphosed
into "the green man"

Before

After

a prototype wild man
or wilderness hybrid
betwixt "civilized" humans
and their primal
            inner
                infidels

which metamorphosed
into the "Blue Man"

and here's how
it all went down

II

The mythology of *das wildermann*
took hold in Arkansas
before it even
became a state

in 1834
a hunting party supposedly saw
"an enormous creature
with 'long locks that fairly
enveloped his neck and shoulders . . .
leaping from twelve to fourteen
feet at a time'"

this was followed in 1856
by reports in the *Caddo Gazette,*
New York Tribune and other papers
of a "stout, athletic man . . . near Texarkana"
attacking a possé from under a lake

a rare sighting
but consistent in description
throughout mucho colonized
regions at the time

(*Crypto-Arkansas,* 55)

in other words
the wild man was the chosen form
for most New World crypto mysteries
of missing links in our midst
harking back to Enkidu

aka
King Gilgamesh's fur-buddy
four thousand years ago

so no wonder the Ozark
oral tradition
hopped on board

especially in the northern Zarks
where the "Missouri Monster"
now known as "Momo"
had a wild blue predecessor
in the Ava environs

(Outpost Liquor and Grocery, Hwy 5, state line)

96 | *Cryptozarkia*

III

"The Blue Man of the Ozarks" or
"The Wild Man of the Ozarks" or
"The Blue Man of Spring Creek" or
"The Blue Man of Howell County"
        first made news
        following the Civil War

in 1865
"a huge, man-like creature . . .
of a purple color . . .
terrorized the countryside . . . .
between the big North Fork
and Spring Creek"

a purported Yankee from St. Louis
known as Solomon Collins
found footprints in the snow
which "were longer and broader than the tracks
of any bear . . . ever seen"

Sol Collins then tracked that beast
all over hell and back
and was eventually led
to "Upper Twin Mountain"   *(Sedalia Weekly Democrat*, Jan 30, 1925)
        only to be met
        by a barrage of boulders

still   Ol' Sol
managed to glimpse a nine foot "figure . . .
the skin of some animal around its waist . . .
covered from head to foot
with a tightly curling coat of short black hair,
which, as the sun struck upon it,
took on a dark blue hue"   (*Springfield Leader*, Nov 17, 1924)

        note: other texts suggest
        the Blue Man "was called that [color]
        for the first man who laid eyes on him,
        Blue Sol Collins"   (Calebandlindapirtle.com)

        who might've received this moniker
        due to his obsessive
                Blue Man tracking
                or because he fought
                with Union forces

but back to the "man-like animal" that   (*Springfield Republican*, June 25, 1915)
"cast aside a great ten-foot club"
                the standard accessory
                of any wild man
                from Renaissance art history

prompting Blue Sol
to assemble a mob
to trace "the tracks
of the giant [and]
. . . The wild man was seen
by many people"   (*Sedalia Weekly Democrat*)

but never shot
and never captured
        or of course
photographed

(*St. Joseph Observer*, July 10, 1915)

(*Washington Times*, July 9, 1915)

(phantomsandmonsters.com)

IV

                 The "Ozark Mountain Freak"
              then reappeared nine years later
                         abducting livestock
                               for a week

            then only appeared sporadically
                      from 1890 to 1910

                            but in 1911
           "his den was found" by Ott Collins
               in a cave near Bryant Creek
               the "floor . . . littered with
                     the bones of animals
                          he had eaten"

                             allegedly
           the "wild man . . . tried to get away
              but was caught and turned over
                          to authorities"

                       an account later
                     refuted in various
                         area papers

still
a resurgence surged in 1915
when "Oc Collins"
"saw the 'Blue Man'
running down a hog in the woods . . .
less robust than" before
his fur now described
"as iron gray"

(*Springfield Republican*)

(*Moberly Weekly Monitor*, Aug 10, 1915)

by "1924,
terror was prevailing over northern Howell and Douglas Counties.
From Tater Hill to Collins Ford
and from Blue Buck to the Ava Crossing
people were searching for the Blue Man"

a report then came in '38
from the Bunt Brothers in Johnson Hollow
whose dogs treed "a man
hissing and snarling in anger . . .
hairy and apparently
blue from the cold"

(phantomsandmonsters.com)

after that
the sightings went ape
thereby framing the Blue Man as
a super-human gorilla-man
according to
the current trend

V

Same thing in Branson
the worst place in the world

unless banjo-Evangel Baptistland/
Mormon-Yakov-Disneyland/
bonanza-boyband-Jesusland
is your cup of tea

that's where the fieldwork began
went up there to find out what
the deal is with
the Blue Man Grill

but guess what
it wasn't there

what was
was a Bigfoot Yeti Amusement Armageddon
of cartoon funhouse bouncy houses
mini-golfed with "monkey jumps"
plus a clamberland of kiddy cages
squealing w/ corona-rides

VI

So I set off for Smallet
to track the Blue Man's original range
exploring the shores of Spring Creek
now populated with beaucoup farms

also   some chatroom chatter I encountered
inspired a search for Scottish names
in nineteenth century cemeteries
since Tom Peters had posted
"I wonder if the Scottish legend
of Blue Men might be part of" recent hype

(*Ozarks Alive*)

to which Harriett Hoffman had replied
"That could be true because
Scottish and Irish people were
the first settlers in this area"

that's why I went searching
even though the Blue Men of Minch
also known as Storm Kelpies
go back to the Moors
and refer to semi-sirens
of African origin

according to history
Scottish Blue Men were mermen
looking for sailors to drown
in the Outer Hebrides

but that didn't mean
distortions never happened
because that's what
always happens

take for example
reports of the Blue Man's club
which vary in size
from six to ten feet
though sometimes morphing
into a "spear"

(*News Leader*, Oct 3, 1965)

not to mention
deviations in attire
sometimes depicting
the beskinned Blue Man as a caveman
with "a breech cloth and shoulder piece
made of skins"

Whatever the case
there were a lot of Civil War
gravesites to be found
the first being Whites
near Table Rock Knob
containing WASPy stock
from the 1880s

including a couple McFarlands
from the Gaelic form of Mac Pharlain
of "the ancient Scottish kingdom of Dalriada"

(houseofnames.com)

next came Dobbs
a graveyard near Iron Mountain
containing a few Elliott infants
from the mid 1800s
a name "of important
Scottish origin"

(irishsurnames.com)

and cruising on
still crossing creeks
I came to Twin Bridges
Campground and Resort
where what I saw
spoke for itself

then shooting up highway
181
I chanced upon the boneyard where
the mystery of the Blue Man
was suddenly
solved

VII

But to be sure
I had to hike up
Twin Mountain
where Blue Sol Collins
had been attacked

so I parked and hoofed it
through the woods
with the sun going down
and the dread setting in

a dread I'd met
while tracking supposed
supernaturals before

knowing what's not possible
yet sweating the tales
told time and again

it's always eerie
crunching through the hush
of nothing rustling
in the brush

the eyes of haints
hanging in the air
gooseflesh rippling
everywhere

just waiting for the final
             screeching
             screeling
           skullbashing
         SMAKK
                signaling
                It's over, Chuck!

(July 10, 1915)

VIII

Past overhangs of icy crust
        limestone bluffs
       random caverns
      and rotting logs

        I couldn't help
          considering
           conjectures

KRUNCH!

like the St. Joseph Observer
     claiming the Blue Man
      was "probably not
        very old"

KRUNCH!

or the Moberly Weekly Monitor
stating "the 'Blue Man'
cannot be expected
to live much longer"
due to getting
whiter and whiter

(Aug 10, 1915)

KRUNCH!

because what do reporters know
about wild man physiology
or Blue Man life expectancy
when bona fide biologists
have never had the chance
to study such a specimen?

KRUNCH!

the result being
I got to the top
and found nothing but
detritus

KRUNCH!

like that caca published
in the Springfield Leader and other papers
claiming some race
of half-Spanish
half-Native
American
mutants

Some years before the American revolution, while Missouri was still a part of the French colony of Louisiana, a French fur trader came into the Ozarks bringing with him a very beautiful Spanish woman. The trader soon tired of his fair companion, bartered her to an Indian chief for a goodly package of furs, and slipped away, leaving the woman a captive. The poor woman thus abandoned in the wilderness, lost her reason, and lived for years a demented creature of the woods.

From her sprang a strange race of people, half Spanish, half Indian. They never mingled with either French or Indians, but hid away in remote and inaccessible places, where they increased in numbers, and were known to exist for many years. When the pioneer settlers poured into the Ozarks from 1820 to 1840 the strange half breed race disappeared, and it was generally supposed by those who knew anything about them, that they migrated into more remote and unsettled depths of the wilderness. The Boston mountains in western Arkansas, were thought to be the place which they had retreated to. From these people, probably the last of their race, came the "Blue Man of Spring Creek." That was

(Nov 17, 1924)

IX

"There are a ton of Collins south of Willow Springs
around a little place called Siloam Springs . . .
to my knowledge, the center of Collins-dom
and interestingly, the local lore is . . .
the Collins are the family that
Daniel Woodrell's novel *Winter's Bone*
is based on."

(text from my buddy Hippy
near Sycamore MO)

"So many Dolly kids were that way,
ruined before they had chin hair, groomed
to live outside square law and abide by the remorseless
blood-soaked commandments that governed lives
led outside square law. There were two hundred Dollys,
plus Lockrums, Boshells, Tankersly, and Langans, who
were basically Dollys by marriage,
living within thirty miles."

(Woodrell,
Winter's Bone, 2006, 8)

"Ree discovers unforeseen depths in herself
and in the Dolly clan—a family network that
protects its own at any cost"

(*Ibid.*, back cover
paperback)

"The Dolly family name was found in the USA,
the UK, Canada and Scotland between 1840 and 1920"

(ancestry.com)

"in Scotland [the name of Dolly]
fell 90 percent
between 1881 and 2014"

(forebears.io/surnames/dolly)

"The Lochrome family name
was found in Scotland in 1901"

(ancestry.com)

"The Boshell family name was found in the USA,
the UK, and Scotland between
1840 and 1920"

(ancestry.com)

Langhan "is of Anglo-Norman descent
spreading to Ireland, Scotland and Wales"

(irishsurnames.com)

                                                    "The Scottish are assholes.
                                                     And I know because
                                                     that's where my family's from"

(Lea Graham, my wife)

           X

But like I said
the question of the Blue Man
had already been resolved
when I stumbled upon

Holmes Flatrock Cemetery
which was chock full
of Scottish folk

primarily those
descended from the "Kollyns"   (*Select Surnames Website*)
"a common name in Scotland"
according to historian
Michael Collins Dunn

who traced a seventeenth century
"variation of MacCollin,
[from the] Gaelic MacCuillin . . . .
transplanted from lowland Scotland"   (tamandmichael.com)
via Ireland
            to the Ozarks

more to the point
this graveyard was just
a few miles shy
of Twin Mountain

and was packed full
of Collinses from
the 1800s

meaning this wasn't the haunt
of some suspect Blue Man
as much as it was the literal turf
of the real ass clan
of the Collins

like Ott   who found the den in 1911
and O.C.   who saw the wild man
               chasing a pig
and those around Collins Ford
who sought the Blue Man in '24

but mostly Blue Sol
who tracked the creature
      "from the watershed between the Big North Fork and Spring Creek . . . .
      following those great foot prints. Far away to the north,
      almost to Indian [C]reek, then in a wi[l]d
      semi-circle to the west,
      until he was close above
      the North [F]ork"   *(Springfield Leader)*

the route I followed
when the fact was now obvious
that this was the land
the Collins had founded
      farmed
      lived
      and died on

meaning Blue Sol
fought the monster
in his own neighborhood

      Aye,
because there never was
a roundabout hunt through hollers
leading some northern trapper with
the unlikely name of Collins
to the hotbed of his relatives
      as if he'd never
      settled it
      his own
      damn
      self

XI

It didn't take much Googling
to find Old Sol Collins
born July 17, 1789
died December 1882
in Washburn Cemetery
Sebastian County
Arkansas

SOLOMON "OLD SOL" COLLINS
JULY 1789 VA
DEC. 1882
MARRIED DELILA NICHOLS OCT. 1. 1812
CLAIRBORNE CO. TENN.
VETERAN
WAR 1812 & CIVIL WAR 1864

as the listing claims
"Solomon was a veteran of the War of 1812
according to the article in the *West Plains Daily Quill*
by Marvin Oaks June 19, 1997"

adding that
"For serving in the war of 1812,
[Sol] was awarded . . . 120 acres
in Douglas County"

with the caveat
"There are many recorded stories about Solomon
in Douglas County History books.
He was a legend"

and now
even more

XII

Because here's what happened
when some wiseacre came along
and decided to add
to that store of stories

by making it seem
like a Collins who settled in Missouri
had never ventured
unto the homeland of his name

where Old Sol and his wife Delila
raised eleven kids as
"the first family in . . .
 Willow Springs Township"

So why the deception?
Because said wiseacre wanted
to memorialize
    mythologize
    and ingrain the family name
    in the family place

so that's exactly what happened
when some conning
            plotting
            Scot or not
            named Collins
            made it happen

because who else
would give a hoot?

Hence
until this thesis can be disproved
this is the most conclusive record
chronicling the Wild Man
of Spring Creek

who roamed the ancestral land
of the descendants of
Old Sol Collins

and who
in the shadow of
Upper Twin Mountain
would've been one
                    spry
                    septuagenarian
when tracking the Blue Man
after "the age
of 77."   (findagrave.com/memorial/39757931)

Crab Tick Canard

Crab Tick Canard

The notorious "crab tick" was called to my attention
at the Fourteenth Annual Ozarks Symposium
at Missouri State University in West Plains

after presenting on hoop snakes and wampular felines
someone from the audience asked
about the mysterious
Mexican crab tick

which can be described
as a plasma sucking parasite
huge enough to desiccate
a full grown
St. Bernard

this launched another
        atypical
        investigation

atypical because
this critter has no connection
to any established
genuine folklore

atypical also
because this myth went viral
in less than a decade

in fact
its origin can be traced back
to "Otus the Head Cat"
a satirical column in *The Arkansas Dem-Gazette*
          from August 9, 2008

as reported by invented human Fischer Wutend
          "The tick was floating past the boat and sucking on a three-pound largemouth bass.
            I took my paddle and whacked it good. It was like smashing a ripe honeydew melon"

          reporter Michael Story
          aka Otus
          went on to note
          how "Hurricane Katrina blew the giant Mexican crab tick
              into south Arkansas almost three years ago"   (arkansasonline.com/news/2008)
          and a federal study
          was under way

a story so popular
it made a comeback in 2012
in an article entitled "Bumper Crop
                    of Giant Crab Ticks Scuttling North"

in which a misleading photograph
clearly showing a king crab
was published along with the information
that "Caridis sanguinantis" was making its way
"as far north as the Ozarks"

Entomologist Andrew Acarina displays a mounted and desiccated giant Mexican crab tick trapped last month on the Wildlife Lane Nature Trail at Millwood State Park

Dr. Acarina   (meaning subclass of small arachnids)
from the Entomology/Etymology Department   (oh no there isn't!)
at South Arkansas Community College
claimed they can "suck five quarts of blood
        out of a human in an hour"   (nwaonline.com/news/2012)
with the recommendation of barbecue tongs
for removing pest

this novelty item
took on a new incarnation in 2014
when arkansasonline.com published
        "Ticks Likely Safe, Even If Hades Froze, Expert Says"

in which "Dr. Apu Nahasapeemapetilon,
        renowned hematologist and director of the University
        of Arkansas' Donald J. Tyson Center"
        weighed in on the infestation

Dr. Apu   (Doh!)

with support from "Ben 'Bubba' Edlund from Hot Springs . . .
owner/operator of the world-famous
Arkansas Tick & Chigger Farm"   (arkansasonline.com/news/2014)
at 845 Whittington Avenue

       which is actually an alligator farm
       /petting zoo
       containing one Jenny Haniver of
       a manufactured merman

nevtheless
the king crab photo
ran again in 2017
in an article entitled "UAMS Researchers
                    Recruiting Citizen Tick-Pickers"

this time   however
Dr. Acarina was now Bubba Edlund
showing off his apocryphal crab tick
displayed @ tick & chigger farm

the weird thing being
this article was serious
in reporting on Lyme disease
                "Rocky Mountain spotted fever,
                tularemia,
                ehrlichiosis"
                et cetera

when all of a sudden
it switched directions
informing us
    "The crab tick's usual diet
    consists of raccoons and other small mammals . . .
    the occasional armadillo and
    rat-tailed smoot"

readers were also informed
that the crab tick "trapped in 2007 . . .
        had been sucking on a young anhinga
        (also called a water turkey)"

reportedly
"200,000 visitors a year
come to see the giant Mexican crab tick"   (arkansasonline.com/news/2017)

beyond that
"the . . . scourge of 2008"   (*NewsBank* and pressreader.com)
received minor mention
in 2018

meanwhile   as always
readers repeated
what they'd read

whether based on actual science or
the standard openly
published disclaimer
that Otus the Cat

was an "award-winning column
of humorous

fabrication."   (nwaonline.com/news/2012)

Hellhounds Abound: Oh the Mendacity!

Hellhounds Abound: Oh the Mendacity!

In Euro and American folklore
there are tons of tales of hellish hounds
dating back to Cerberus
Greek Guardian of the Underworld/
Hound of Hades with three heads

but in the Ozarks
I'm only concerned
with traditional black "booger dogs"
of extra wolflike proportions
in the southeast corner
of the Show-Me state

the "great ghost dog" of McDonald County
comes to mind
chronicled by Vance Randolph
as "bigger than a cow"

so does that "great black dog"
in turn of the century Taney County
which ran alongside a messenger of death
whose riding whip "slashed right through"
its massive silhouette

plus that one near Galena
seen walking with a phantom man
and vanishing
sporadically

but especially
there's the story of a hermit named Wolf/e
who was lying on his deathbed when
       "a bolt of lightning . . . set
         the house on fire [and] . . .
         A strange black dog slipped out . . .
         from under the sick man's bed"

(Ozark Magic and Folklore,
224–226; 275)

         a myth harking back to Old Shuck
         an East Anglian devil dog
         who broke into a church in 1577
         during a lightning storm
             "resulting in the deaths of
             four worshippers"

(BBC.com)

What all these legends have in common
is the buzz that if someone
sees such escorts to "the other side"
three times
       the accursed shall be
dead on the morrow

but there's also the electrical theme
that hellhounds are charged by thunderstorms
so are usually seen
following a rain

which made it the right time
to head up to Springfield
where the Nixa Hellhound
has been spooking locals
for decades

Ie, Mikayla in Ozark 2009
recounting how her and her mother
saw what "looked like
            a deer and a dog . . .
            had a one-night stand"

its chatroom description
matching that of Sgttork's in 2010
who allegedly fled
a hellhound as

xXsweetcandyXx did in 2012
when "glowing red eyes,
            and a black coat"
almost made her
pee her pants

likewise   in 2015
"'Tweedy Jo' Custer" and his cousin
witnessed "a black flash
            that looked like a really big dog . . .
            mean as hell . . . like a big feral hog"

 (nixahellhound.blogspot.com)

The common denom of all these sightings
being hype pumped up
by a couple morning
DJ personalities
on Power 96.5

who circa April Fools 2009
even dubbed their demon "Paul"

leading to a Facebook page
documenting helldog encounters
aligning highway 65
from Ozark down
to the Arkansas line

But like I said
it was the right time to head that way
since a storm had come through
the previous eve

my first stop being
the old Winoka Camp
built on the site of a hunting lodge
        "founded around 1890
          on the James River"

where with the mud still moist
from the night before
canine tracks
were found on the trails
        but none larger
          than a schnauzer

the infamous massacre camp   however
where "several girl scouts were brutally murdered"
was fenced off and screened in
to keep people from seeing in

this is where Paul was photographed
taking a bath
by birdwatcher Louis Herman

(*Fair City News*, Oct 30, 2009)

a picture so blurry &
suspiciously Photochopped
that it can only be compared to
and/or trusted as much
as the other sketchy photograph
of Paul clearly
being a deer

(Paul's FB page)

No doubt
this hellhound's stomping grounds
were inspired by fire

like the one that burned down St. Mary's Church
back in medieval England
as well as the conflagration
which torched the Winoka Lodge
sometime in the seventies

      thereby inviting
      urban legend speculation
      of girl scout slaughter

      an incident that actually occurred
      near Locust Grove Oklahoma
      1977

            (note: there was no "Albino
            Farm" either)

So I shot on down to Highway JJ
where back in 2018
Amie Jo Baer reported
a pack of marauding
"huge black wolve dogs"   (spiritseekerblog.org)

      but driving that road
twice at dusk
the only thing I really saw
was me being
an utter fool

I mean Duh!
everyone knows
this junk is bunk
but there I was
following up

then driving back to Arkansas
with no new news
and no new clues
other than the same
                  old
                       crock of rot

injecting something
           supernatural
into the Southern
Midwestern
mundane.

Kraken Down on the Oklahoma Octopus

Kraken Down on the Oklahoma Octopus

Tentacle 1

In the western extremities
of the Ozark range

    a rusty brown
    horse-sized
    man-eating
    mollusk

        has been making news
        for centuries

The lore of North
American tribes
however

    is not specific
    to any ident
    ifiable culture

        If anything
        it's the myth of the myth
        we hear about

           and what it's about
           is a homicidal
           bloodsucking
           leachlike
           spirit

So let's get
past that
and establish that

reports of its current
incarnation
are endemic to
three manmade reservoirs:

Oolagah
Thunderbird
and Tenkiller

all of which
never existed
before 19
65

after which
various rumors
of humans pulled under

and/or discovered
with suction scars

began to surface

Tentacle 2

As the article "Oklahoma Octopus
and the Myth Behind This Name"
states

    "many people believe
     that the high mortality rate
     and a large number of unexplained drownings . . .

     are a clear indication of its presence.
     There have also been
     numerous sightings"   (pittypets.com)

         as explained in
         "Killer Oklahoma Octopus Vies to Become
         the Heartland's Loch Ness Monster"

           "the average person at the lake
            sucks down around a case of Bud Light
            throughout the day"   (zimbio.com)

an exaggeration   but to the point
that partying has played its part
in spawning mass
speculation

         Still   there's absolutely "no
         known physical evidence"   (*Tahlequah Daily Press*)
         or credible accounts
         anywhere

no real names
no real dates
no photos no
medical or
police reports

just pure
old fashioned
narratives

doing what
they do

Tentacle 3

What we do have is *Tentacles*
the worst Hollywood B movie
to ever insult
filmmaking

    released in 1977
    to capitalize on *Jaws* fever
    this spaghetti western
    produced travesty

        of octo stock
        footage fused
        with crap edits

            of Henry Fonda
            John Huston
            and Shelley Winters

                was so sloppy that
                America rejected it

                denied it
                forgot it
                and forced it out
                of memory

                    But one thing
                    that couldn't be expunged

                        is that horripilating tentacles
                        have an enduring grip

that is
there's just something so
fearfully foreign

      in the imagery of octopi
      berserking out on
      swimming kids

that sheer fear triggers
alien terror

Which of course
was the horror du jour
in that splash & slash era of
from the deep blockbusters
ranging from

Piranah   (1978)
to *The Deep*   (1977)
to *Jaws 2*   (1978)
to *Orca* and other   (1977)
frightmare scenarios

      designed to fulfil
      a trendy brown
      your pants demand

at a time when Cold War scapegoatings
left us with no Viet Cong
to single out
for our sins

meaning
instead of looking across waters
for demons to stigmatize
we xeno-projected
into on our own

    so no wonder the idea
    of a subaquatic anomaly
    grabbling and grappling
    latched onto
    our consciousness

in other words
the stage
was set

Tentacle 4

Hence
hoaxes arose
where octopi
never go

    for example
    there are no known
    squidular species
    "found in freshwater"   *(ABC Science*, 2013)

        but an "octopus was found dead . . .
        in Watts Bar Lake near Chattanooga"   (Associated Press, April 5, 2010)
        during this
        millennium

and ironically
in Arkansas 2003
on Lake Conway
where I live

biologists believe
these *Octos vulgari*
were abandoned from aquariums

but not in the case
of Grand Lake
in the northeast corner
of the Sooner state

according to FOX23
"Someone reportedly
 threw [one] into the water
 as part of a joke"
in '017

to which some punk named Owen Bruse
commented on Facebook
"im actually the one
 who found [it]"

                (and judging by him flipping bird
                in photo profile
                it'd be no surprise to find
                he did the dirty deed)

whereas yacht club manager Brian Stengel
replied "I saw it
personally

but it was dead and had
been used as a center peace
to a seafood buffet"   (facebook.com/fox23news/posts)

                        neither of these witnesses   though
                        would reply to FB messenger

                but as editor Amie Cato-Remer
                of *Vian Tenkiller News*
                affirmed in an email

                        "I am the one who wrote the story . . .
                        The 'octopus' was actually caught
                        [in] LAKE TENKILLER"

Tentacle 5

Point being
the literature is full
of consistent in
consistencies

    like Cato-Remer adding
    it was found "in an area called Chicken Creek"   (email, July 15, 2022)
    vs. Brian Stengel specifying
    "Duck Creek"   (facebook.com/fox23news/posts)

still
the OK Octopus
became recognized by the mainstream
as the official state crypto critter
shortly after
2013

    especially on commercial maps
      like DanMeth's *North American Cryptids* and   (2014)
    Poster Foundry's
      Folklore and Supernatural Phenomena and   (2020)
    Hog Island Press'
      Monsters in America, Vol. 2   (2021)

      for one reason
      and one reason only:

episode 5
of *Lost Tapes*
broadcast back
in 2009

thus
author Denver Michaels
echoes others:

"nearly everything involving the Oklahoma Octopus
can be directly traced back"
   to this Animal Planet show

      adding
"be it intentional or coincidental,
   the events depicted . . . have become recorded
as 'fact' and used as 'evidence'"

*(People Are Seeing
Something,* 2022)

            Researcher Zafar Iqbal
               redebunks and agrees:
      "The online discussions and articles I found
         were from after [2009] . . .
      Nothing came up when I searched
      before 2008"

(pittypets.com)

which I can confirm
and so can you
by doing a simple
Google search

Main takeaway:
a fictional reenactment
designed for entertainment
spectacularized and mesmerized
chatrooms full of chatterers who

    believed what
    they wanted to believe

      thereby adding
      an explosive
        internet
        element

          that took off
          like wildfire

Tentacle 6

So once again there I was
literally fishing
for something everyone
knows is nonsense

    but that's what you gotta do
    in a cryptozoo investigation
    to test the scientific theory
    and dig up a backstory

I was on Tenkiller Lake in my motorboat
my anchor rope was 48 feet
and my bait was
frozen shad

    the wind was blowing
    at a pretty good clip
    with one foot waves
    bouncing the bow

        having interviewed two local cashiers
        who'd never heard
        of Das Octo
        and two others
        who couldn't be bothered

          I was a skeptic

        when suddenly
        the boat swung free
        and I pulled up 42 feet
        of lacerated line

           prompting a wiggle
           to squiggle thru skin

              The gnawing grind
              of sharp submerged
                  under-rocks

              or Oklahoma
              Octopus?

Tentacle 7

Popular t-shirt
at Burnt Cabin Marina gift shop
on west side of lake:

> "Weekend Forecast:
>   Boating with a Chance
> of Drinking"

Popular t-shirt
at Oklahoma Station store
on north side of lake:

> "Day Drinking on Lake Tenkiller
>   Is My Happy Place"

Sticker purchased at the latter:

Conclusion being:

merchandise mongers in environs
are invested in pumping up
an already established
booze abuse culture

responsible for
"a high number of . . .
 unexplained disappearances"   (tocontriveandjive.wordpress.com)

    Case in point:
    our neighbors in Cabin #1
    chugging breakfast beer
    then hitting lake
    for water ski
    whoopery

        as do
        hundreds of boaters
        a percentage of which
        drunkenly drown

            causing others
            to blame it on
            a cephalopod

        a nonviolent
        "intelligent and sentient
         organism that experiences . . .
         the same problems and desires"
        as us   (qtd. in "Science and the Making of
                         My Octopus Teacher")

including extreme emotions
and interspecies
empathy

Tentacle 8

But then there's the fact

that those who document
and deconstruct
and disseminate
solid
credible
information

also spread
disinformation

it's just unavoidable
as *Lost Tapes* demonstrates
as well as every publication and production
questioning cryptids
including this

and that's the rub
to comment or not
when objective research
will be perverted

cuz that's the nature
of our nature

in this new
supercharged age

    of *click click click*
    conspiracy theory
    no accountability
    and total bullshite

        compounding the way
        it's always been.

List of Images

Note: The author has assumed responsibility for acquisition of image permissions in this text, in which the "Fair Use" clause of International Copyright Law protects scholarship serving a "socially useful purpose" (in this case, by exposing narratives that encourage trespassing, misinformation, needless absurdity, and outright lunacy).

Figure 1: Big Al illustration copyright © 2021 Mark Spitzer.

Figure 2: Ozark Howler illustration copyright © 2021 Bogel Bear.

Figure 3: Ozark Howler photograph courtesy of *Phantoms & Monsters* 2022.

Figure 4: Nieces and mauled tree photograph copyright © 2021 Mark Spitzer.

Figure 5: Giant catfish photograph courtesy of Riverbender.com 2022.

Figure 6: *Amazing Stories,* Vol. 19, no. 1, 1945 cover in public domain.

Figure 7: Destany Lytle photograph copyright © 2021 Felisha Martin, courtesy of Destany Lytle.

Figure 8: Author, Ben "Minnow Bucket" Damgaard and Gene Damgaard photograph copyright © 2021 Destany Lytle.

Figure 9: Blowing Cave map image from *Shavertron,* Vol. 2 courtesy of Richard Toronto 2022.

Figure 10: Blowing Cave map image courtesy of Association for Arkansas Cave Studies 2022.

Figure 11: Kayla Sapkota in the Meat Grinder, photograph copyright © 2021 Chad Holderfield, courtesy of Ben "Minnow Bucket" Damgaard.

Figure 12: Salamander photograph copyright © 2021 Mark Spitzer.

Figure 13: Stalactites photograph copyright © 2021 Mark Spitzer.

Figure 14: Moist formations photograph copyright © 2021 Mark Spitzer.

Figure 15: Waterfall photograph copyright © 2021 Destany Lytle.

Figure 16: Smiling corona virus image copyright © 2022 Mark Spitzer.

Figure 17: Jack of the green photograph copyright © 2019 Mark Spitzer.

Figure 18: Green man. Photograph of illustration copyright © British Library Board acquired 2022 from *Book of Hours* (*Bedford Hours*) circa 1410–1430, folio 9r.

Figure 19: A wild man of the woods illustration copyright © Science Photo Library acquired 2022.

Figure 20: Momo sculpture photograph copyright © 2022 Mark Spitzer.

Figure 21: Blue Man Grill photograph copyright © 2022 Mark Spitzer.

Figure 22: Yeti Zone image copyright © 2022 Mark Spitzer.

Figure 23: Blue Man cartoon used with permission of *Springfield News-Leader* 2022, originally published October 3, 1965.

Figures 24 & 25: Momo photographs copyright © 2022 Mark Spitzer.

Figure 26: Excerpt from *Springfield Leader* used with permission of *Springfield News-Leader* 2022, originally published November 17, 1924.

Figures 27–30: Gravestone photographs copyright © 2022 Mark Spitzer.

Figure 31: Old Sol Collins' gravestone photograph from findagrave.com copyright © 2019 Richard Meador.

Figure 32: Crab tick photograph image copyright © 2006 *Seattle Times*. Original caption was "Darryl Pederson, head of Keyport Foods, displays a king crab caught in the Barents Sea, which is in the upper right-hand corner of the map behind him. The crabs were introduced to the Barents Sea from the Pacific waters of the Russian Far East in the 1960s. (Photo by Steve Ringman)."

Figure 33: Apu Nahasapeemapetilon image copyright © 2022 Photo 12 / Alamy Stock Photo.

Figure 34: Hot Springs Merman photograph copyright © 2019 courtesy of Arkansas Alligator Farm and Petting Zoo, alligatorfarmzoo.com.

Figures 35 & 36: Nixa Hellhound photographs from Paul's Facebook page courtesy of Dawn McClain 2022.

Figure 37: Tentacles US poster, 1977 image copyright © 1977 / Alamy Stock Photo.

Figure 38: Lake Conway Octopus photograph copyright © 2003 courtesy of Arkansas Game and Fish Commission.

Figure 39: Sticker photograph copyright © 2022 Mark Spitzer.

Author photo: copyright © 2018 Amelia LaMair.

About the Author

Mark Spitzer is the author of thirty-one books ranging from environmental nonfiction to novels to memoirs to literary translations to collections of poetry and essays on teaching writing. Specific publications include *Crypto-Arkansas* (Spuyten Duyvil), *GLURK! A Hellbender Odyssey* (Anaphora), *In Search of Monster Fish* (University of Nebraska Press), and *Investigative Creative Writing* (Equinox). Having been a professor of creative writing at Truman State University and the University of Central Arkansas, he now searches for amphibians and wild fungi in New York's Hudson Valley while simultaneously inhabiting the legendary Haint of the Green-Haired Freak forever paddling Ozark creeks. For more info visit *sptzr.net*.